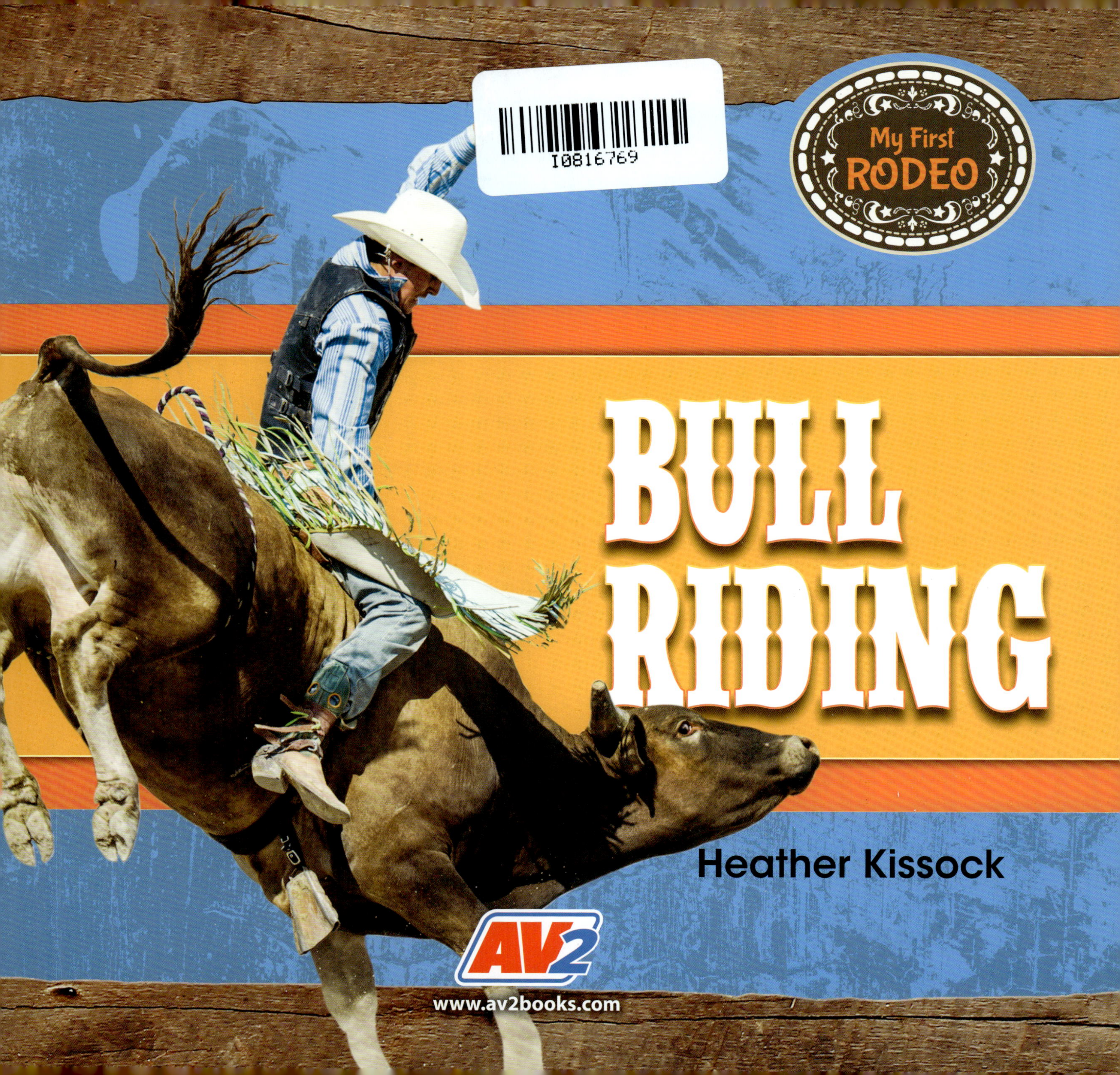
I0816769
My First
RODEO
BULL
RIDING
Heather Kissock
AV2
www.av2books.com

Step 1
Go to **www.av2books.com**

Step 2
Enter this unique code
ZLAJYQ4JI

Step 3
Explore your interactive eBook!

AV2
My First RODEO
BULL RIDING
Start!

AV2 is optimized for use on any device

Your interactive eBook comes with...

Audio
Listen to the entire book read aloud

Videos
Watch informative video clips

Weblinks
Gain additional information for research

Try This!
Complete activities and hands-on experiments

Key Words
Study vocabulary, and complete a matching word activity

Quizzes
Test your knowledge

Slideshows
View images and captions

View new titles and product videos at www.av2books.com

BULL RIDING

Contents

I am going to my first rodeo. I want to watch the bull riding event.

The **first** bull riding events were held in Mexico in the **1500s**. They were called *jaripeos*.

I sit in the stands with my family. The arena is in front of us. This is where the cowboys ride the bulls.

3.43
BlueDEF
PBR Rewards
NORTRAX

I see the first cowboy get on his bull. He is dressed to ride.

The spurs on the cowboy's boots help him stay on the bull.

A helmet keeps the cowboy's head safe.

His vest helps to protect
his chest and back.

He wears a glove
on his riding hand.

Chaps cover his legs.

The cowboy slips his hand into a rope that is wrapped around the bull. He ties the rope around his hand.

The **bull rope** is the **only support** a rider has during a ride.

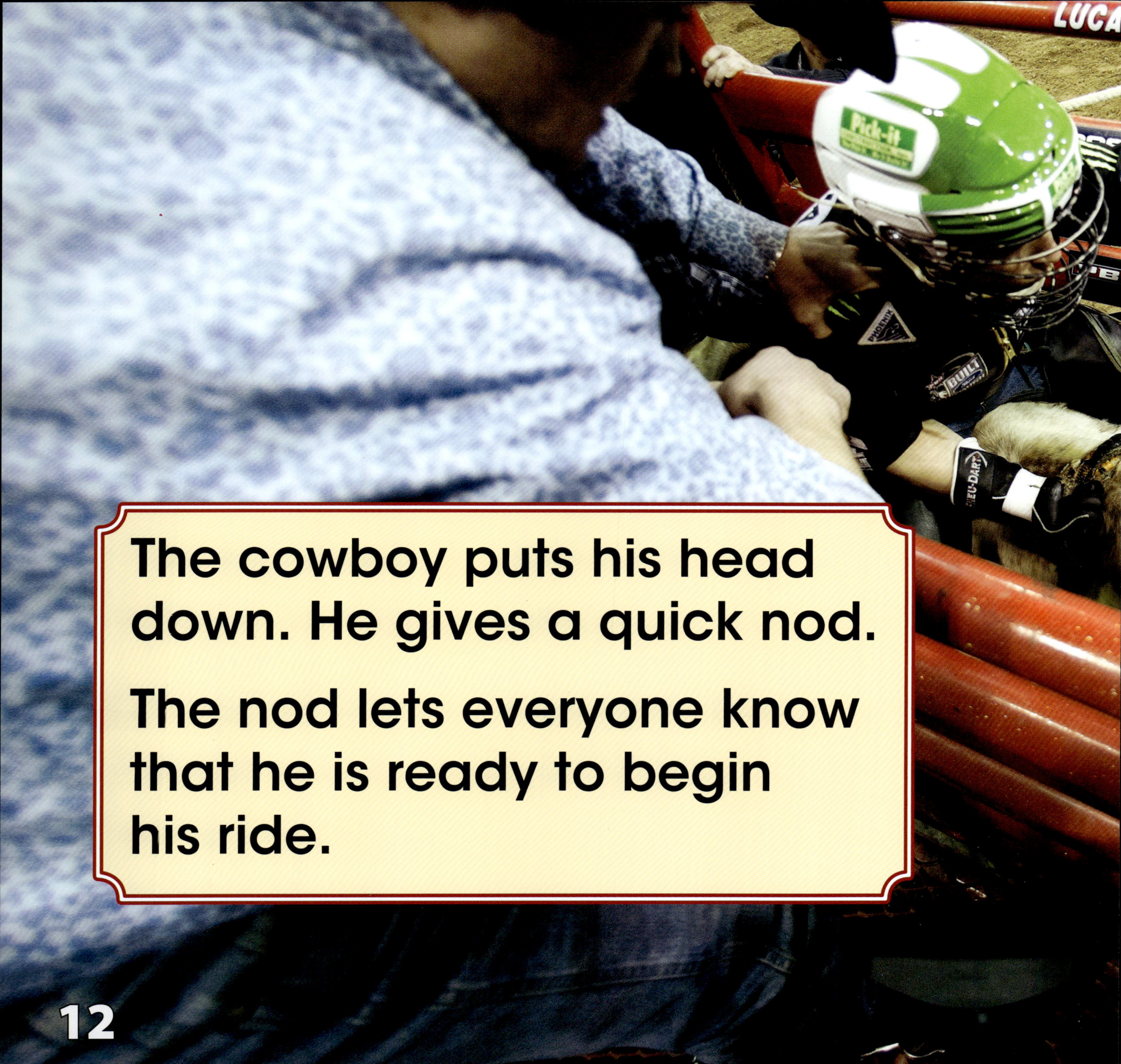

The cowboy puts his head down. He gives a quick nod.

The nod lets everyone know that he is ready to begin his ride.

Wrangler
FORD F-SERIES
LAS VEGAS
DEWALT
LAS VEGAS
BUILT FORD TOUGH
FORD F-SERIES
Wrangler
CBS SPORTS NETWORK
LAS VEGAS
ARIAT
LINCOLN WELDERS
FORD

Joseph F
Excavating,
BUILDER

The bull charges into the arena. He bucks and spins.

The cowboy holds tight, with one hand in the air. He knows that he will be scored on how well he rides the bull.

Eight seconds pass. A bell sounds. The cowboy lets go of the rope. He jumps off the bull.

The rider **must stay** on the bull for **eight seconds** or the ride does not count.

MURPHY'S

WYOMING
WYOMING
Justin
BOOTS
ROUGHY
MONTANA
SILVERSMITHS

A clown runs between the cowboy and the bull. He helps the bull leave the arena.

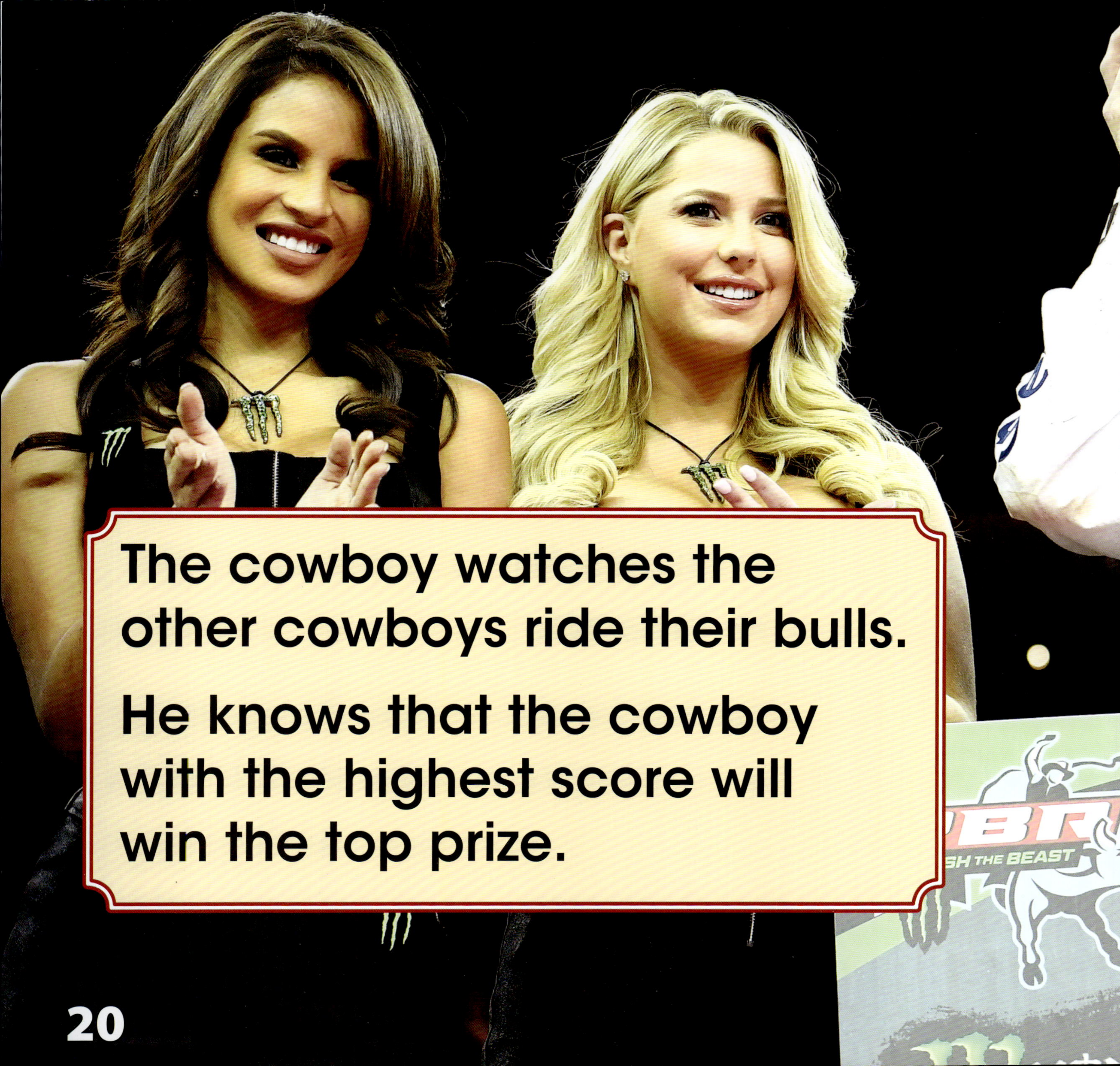

The cowboy watches the other cowboys ride their bulls.

He knows that the cowboy with the highest score will win the top prize.

JANUARY 6, 2019
y to the
der of:
$100,000

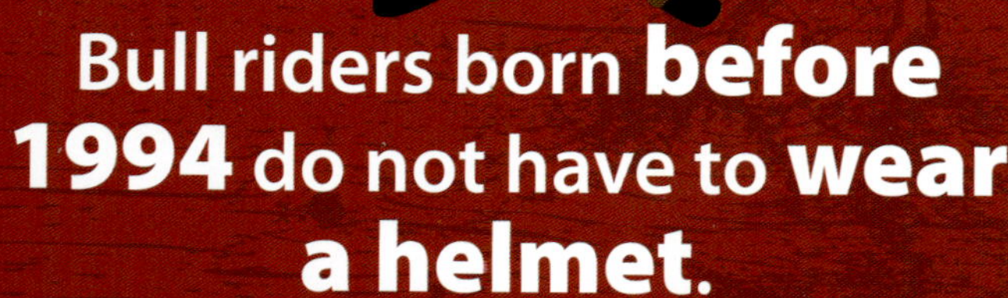

Bull riders born **before 1994** do not have to **wear a helmet**.

A bull named **Red Rock** bucked off more than **300 riders**. Only **1 person** ever lasted **8 seconds** on him.

The **padding** in some bull riding vests is **10 times stronger** than steel.

A bull rider can make **more than $7 million** during his or her career.

A bull can **weigh** as much as **2,000 pounds** (907 kilograms). That is about the same weight as a small car.

A rider can only use **1 hand** to ride the bull. The other hand **must** be **kept in the air**.

KEY WORDS

Research has shown that as much as 65 percent of all written material published in English is made up of 300 words. These 300 words cannot be taught using pictures or learned by sounding them out. They must be recognized by sight. This book contains 81 common sight words to help young readers improve their reading fluency and comprehension. This book also teaches young readers several important content words, such as proper nouns. These words are paired with pictures to aid in learning and improve understanding.

Page	Sight Words First Appearance
4	am, first, I, my, the, to, want, watch
5	in, they, were
6	family, is, of, this, us, where, with
8	get, he, help, him, his, on, see
9	a, and, back, hand, head, keeps
10	around, has, into, only, that
12	begin, down, gives, know, lets, puts
15	air, be, how, one, well, will
16	does, for, go, must, not, off, or, seconds, sounds
19	between, leave, runs
20	other, their
22	before, do, ever, have, more, named, than
23	about, as, can, car, her, make, much, same, small, some, times, use

Page	Content Words First Appearance
4	event, rodeo
5	*jaripeos*, Mexico
6	arena, bulls, cowboys, stands
8	boots, spurs
9	chaps, chest, glove, helmet, legs, vest
10	ride, rider, rope, support
12	nod
16	bell
19	clown
20	prize, score
22	helmet, person, Red Rock
23	career, padding, steel

Published by AV2
276 5th Avenue, Suite 704 #917
New York, NY 10001
Website: www.av2books.com

Library of Congress Cataloging-in-Publication Data
Names: Kissock, Heather, author.
Title: Bull riding / Heather Kissock.
Description: New York, NY : AV2, [2021] | Series: My first rodeo | Audience: Ages 5-8 | Audience: Grades K-1
Identifiers: LCCN 2020004210 (print) | LCCN 2020004211 (ebook) | ISBN 9781791123642 (library binding) | ISBN 9781791123659 (paperback) | ISBN 9781791123666 | ISBN 9781791123673
Subjects: LCSH: Bull riding--Juvenile literature. | Rodeos--Juvenile literature.
Classification: LCC GV1834.45.B84 K57 2021 (print) | LCC GV1834.45.B84 (ebook) | DDC 791.84--dc23
LC record available at https://lccn.loc.gov/2020004210
LC ebook record available at https://lccn.loc.gov/2020004211

Printed in Guangzhou, China
2 3 4 5 6 7 8 9 0 26 25 24 23 22

052022
040522

Project Coordinator: Heather Kissock Designer: Ana María Vidal

AV2 acknowledges Getty, iStock, Shutterstock, and Alamy as the primary image suppliers for this title.